KERNEL TWO

WORKBOOK
Alan C McLean   Robert O'Neill

Longman

Longman Group Limited
*Longman House, Burnt Mill, Harlow,
Essex CM20 2JE, England
and Associated Companies throughout the World.*

© *Longman Group Limited 1983
All rights reserved; no part of this publication
may be reproduced, stored in a retrieval system
or transmitted in any form or by any means, electronic,
mechanical, photocopying, recording or otherwise,
without the prior written permission of the Publishers.*

First published 1983
Fifth impression 1985
ISBN 0 582 51659 5

Illustrated by Peter Dennis, John Fraser, Charles Front
and Snoots Advertising Ltd.

Set in 10/12 Monophoto 2000 Photina

Produced by Longman Group (FE) Ltd
Printed in Hong Kong

Contents

	page		page
Unit one	2	Unit Ten	29
Unit Two	5	Unit Eleven	32
Unit Three	8	Unit Twelve	35
Unit Four	11	Unit Thirteen	38
Unit Five	14	Unit Fourteen	41
Unit Six	17	Unit Fifteen	44
Unit Seven	20	Unit Sixteen	47
Unit Eight	23	Unit Seventeen	50
Unit Nine	26		

Note

This Workbook contains material for further practice in reading and writing of the language presented in *Kernel Two*. The material is arranged in seventeen units corresponding with the units of the Students' Book, and it consists of a variety of exercises to reinforce the structures, functions and vocabulary of *Kernel Two*.

Students should write their answers to the exercises in this Workbook. However, the symbol indicates where lengthier answers need to be written on either a separate piece of paper or on the ruled paper at the back of this Workbook. Answers to the fill-in exercises can be found on pp i–iv. These pages can be pulled out from the centre of the book.

Unit One

1 What happened?

Look at this headline:

Gunmen shoot President Mbongo

What happened?

Yesterday gunmen shot President Mbongo.

Now look at these headlines. Write down what happened yesterday.

1 Brazil beats England 5–0

Yesterday Brazil __*beat*__ England by __*5 goals*__ to nil.

2 Miners walk out of pay talks

Yesterday miners __*walked out*__ of talks about pay.

3 Police arrest 23 at rock concert

Yesterday the __*police*__ arrested twenty-three __*people*__ at a rock concert.

4 Grey wins tenth tennis title

Jack Grey __*won*__ his __*tenth*__ tennis title at Wimbledon.

2 Choose the headline

Read this newspaper story:

> Yesterday thieves broke into the Royal Institute and stole a Bertorelli painting worth £100,000. Police are still looking for the thieves, but so far have made no arrests. Meanwhile, the Director of the Royal Institute, Sir Harold Cassock, has offered a reward of £10,000 for the return of the painting. 'We want it back very badly', said Sir Harold last night.
>
> *The Bertorelli, worth £100,000.*

Now choose the best headline (A, B, C or D) for this story.

A **Director steals painting**

B **Director offers reward**

C **Bertorelli stolen from institute**

D **Police recover missing painting**

The best headline is *Director offers Reward!* (B)

Unit One

3 What kind of hair?

Look at these people. Describe their hair. Use one word for each person. Choose words from those in the box.

| short   long   curly   straight   dark   bald |

1 Joy has got *long curly* hair.   2 Harry is *bald.*

3 Denny has got very *short dark* hair.   4 Polly has got *long dark straight* hair.

4 Wanted

Read this news item:
Police today are looking for a man called Terry Nelson. He has got a moustache, long black hair and a scar on his right cheek.

Now look at these pictures. Which of these men (A, B, C or D) is Terry Nelson?

Terry Nelson is *B.*

Unit One

5 Describe yourself

Look at Thomas Farley's letter to his pen-friend:

My name is Thomas Farley and I come from Richmond. I'm 15 years old and I'm 1.65 metres tall. I've got straight brown hair and I wear glasses.

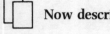 Now describe yourself in the same way.

6 I don't believe it!

Read this conversation between John and Martha. They are talking about flying saucers.

JOHN: I don't believe in flying saucers.
MARTHA: But that boy saw one. It landed in a field and two people got out.
JOHN: I don't believe it! It isn't true. It can't be. There aren't any flying saucers.
MARTHA: A lot of people believe in them, you know.
JOHN: What?
MARTHA: Flying saucers. A lot of people believe in them.
JOHN: That's right. A lot of stupid people.
MARTHA: No, but perhaps they're right. Perhaps there are people on other planets. Perhaps they have landed there. Perhaps they want to speak to us. John!
JOHN: What?
MARTHA: Are you listening to me?
JOHN: No. What are you talking about?
MARTHA: Oh, you never listen to me!

Now look at these statements. Put a tick (√) if they are right, and a cross (×) if they are wrong.

1 John believes in flying saucers. ×
2 A boy saw a flying saucer. √
3 MARTHA: Flying saucers might be true. √
4 JOHN: Only stupid people believe in them. √
5 MARTHA: The people in flying saucers don't want to speak to us. ×
6 John is listening to Martha. ×

Unit Two

1 Likes and dislikes

Look at this table:

	listening to music	watching television	going for walks	reading books
Sue	+ +	+	− −	+
Bill	+	+	−	− −
Joy	−	+	+ +	+ +
Alex	−	− −	+	+ +
You	+	+	+ +	+ +

Key
+ + = loves
+ = quite likes
− = doesn't like
− − = hates

Read about Sue:
Sue loves listening to music. She quite likes watching television and reading books, but she hates going for walks.

Now read about Bill and Joy:
Bill quite likes listening to music and watching television. But he doesn't like going for walks and he hates reading books.

Joy doesn't like listening to music but she loves reading books and going for walks. She quite likes watching television.

Now fill in the table with + and − signs for Bill and Joy.

Look at the table again. Write about Alex's likes and dislikes.

Alex loves _reading books_ ,

but he hates _watching TV_ .

He _quite likes_ going for walks,

but he _doesn't like_ listening to music.

 2 What I like

Use + and − signs to complete the table in exercise 1 with your own likes and dislikes. Then write two or three sentences about them.

Unit Two

3 Ask Sheila

Clive asks Sheila to go to the concert. He says: *Would you like to go to the concert?*
Now you ask Sheila to do these things:

1 Ask her to come outside. — *Would you like to come outside?*

2 Ask her to have a seat. — *Would you like to have a seat? " " " sit down?*

3 Ask her to have a drink. — *Would you like a drink?*

4 Ask her to play tennis on Sunday. — *Would you like to play tennis on Sunday?*

5 Ask her to go for a walk tomorrow. — *Would you like to go for a walk tomorrow?*

4 Free-time crossword

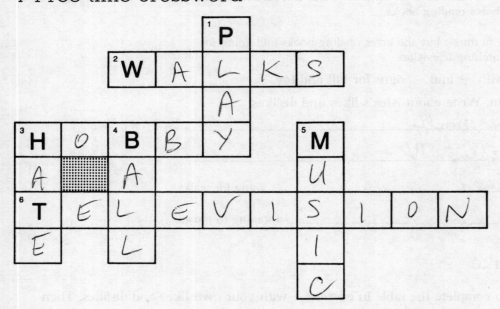

Across
2 We like to go for long *walks* in the country sometimes.
3 Charles likes sky-diving. It's his favourite *hobby*.
6 Don't you get tired of watching *TV*?

Down
1 Does Donald *play* tennis?
3 I don't like horror movies. In fact, I really *hate* them.
4 Did you kick the *ball* into my garden?
5 I like listening to *music*, but I can't play it.

6

Unit Two

5 Choosing a film

Look at this cinema advertisement. Now mark these sentences right (√) or wrong (×).

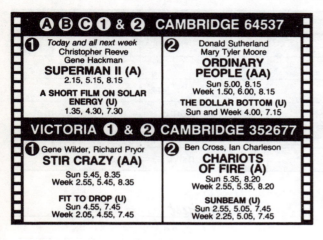

1 *Superman II* is on at the ABC 1. __√__
2 *Ordinary People* is on at the ABC 2. __√__
3 Gene Hackman is in it. __×__
4 Christopher Reeve is in *Superman II*. __√__
5 *Chariots of Fire* is on at the Victoria 1. __×__
6 The other film at the Victoria 1 is *Sunbeam*. __×__
7 *Stir Crazy* starts at 2.55 on Sunday. __×__
8 To book a seat at the Victoria, phone Cambridge 352677. __√__

6 Ask the questions

Claire Walton is interviewing Henry Blake, who worked on the film *Chariots of Fire*. Read the interview and complete Claire's questions.

CLAIRE: What is *Chariots of Fire* about?

HENRY: It's about two British runners in the 1924 Olympic Games. They were very different from each other, but both wanted to win their races. And they did.

CLAIRE: Are you very ¹__interested__ in sport?

HENRY: I'm quite interested in sport because you can learn a lot about people through sport.

CLAIRE: How ²__long__ did it take to make the ³__film__?

HENRY: It took about six months to make. But we had to work for a year before that to find the money to make the film.

CLAIRE: ⁴__How__ ⁵__much__ money did the film ⁶__cost__?

HENRY: It cost about £3 million to make.

CLAIRE: ⁷__What__ are you going to ⁸__do__ now?

HENRY: I finished another film last month, so now I'm going on holiday for a few weeks.

CLAIRE: Well, I hope you have a good holiday. Thank you for talking to us.

HENRY: It was a pleasure.

Unit Three

1 Making comparisons

Look:

	-er	-est	more	most
poor	poorer	poorest	—	—
big	bigger	biggest	—	—
easy	easier	easiest	—	—
handsome	handsomer	handsomest	more handsome	most handsome
difficult	—	—	more difficult	most difficult
expensive	—	—	more expensive	most expensive

Write in the missing words in these sentences:

1 Howard Hughes was the (*rich*) man in the world. _richest_
2 But he wasn't the (*happy*) man in the world. _happiest_
3 And he wasn't the (*handsome*). _most handsome_
4 Or the (*attractive*). _most attractive_
5 Rich people aren't always (*happy*) than poor people. _happier_
6 Perhaps it's (*difficult*) for rich people to be happy. _more difficult_
7 Perhaps it's (*good*) to be poor than to be rich. _better_

2 Which dictionary?

Look at these dictionaries:

 £7.95 1,400 pages 120,000 words

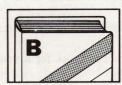 £6.50 1,020 pages 40,000 words

 £5.95 1,200 pages 55,000 words

Now answer these questions:

1 Which dictionary is the most expensive? _A is_
2 Which dictionary is the cheapest? _C is_
3 Which has the most words? _A has_
4 Which is the smallest? _B is_
5 Which dictionary would you buy and why? _A because it is better value for money._

8

Unit Three

3 Ask and tell

Look:

> Ask Sue to open the window: Would you open the window, please?
> Tell Sue to open the window: Open the window, please.

Now ask or tell Jack to do these things:

1 Ask him to come in. — *Would you come in, please?*

2 Tell him to shut the door. — *Shut the door, please.*

3 Ask him to come over here. — *Would you come over here, please?*

4 Tell him to sit down. — *Sit down, please.*

5 Ask him to tell you his name. — *Would you tell me your name, please?*

6 Tell him to read these letters on the wall. — *Read these letters on the wall, please.*

7 Ask him to stop reading. — *Would you stop reading, please?*

8 Tell him to close his eyes. — *Close your eyes, please.*

4 Where is he?

Look at these four places. Where do you think Jack is? Tick the right picture.

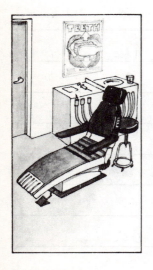   

a _____   b _____   c __✓__ *at the optician's.*   d _____

Unit Three

5 Claire's diary

Look at Claire's diary for tomorrow:

> **Thursday   21st May**
> 9am: interview Jane Ryan
> — Phone Eric
> 11am: 'News in Focus' meeting
> 12.30pm: lunch — Judith
> 7.30pm: yoga class
> 10pm: watch 'Casablanca' TV

Now write about what Claire says she is going to do tomorrow:

1 First I'm going to interview Jane Ryan.

2 Then I'm going to phone Eric.

3 At eleven o'clock I'm going to go to a meeting about the "News in Focus."

4 Then at half-past twelve I'm going to have lunch with Judith.

5 In the evening at 7.30 p.m. I'm going to go to my yoga class.

6 Then 10 p.m. I'm going to watch "Casablanca" on TV.

Unit Four

1 My job

Read what these people say about working for Metrostar, a big company:

My name is Ron Lock. I've been a van driver with the company for two years. It's not a bad job, I suppose, but it's a bit boring at times. The money's quite good – I made £8,000 last year. £10,000

I'm Pat Jenkins, I'm personnel manager for Metrostar. I've been here since 1980. I love my job – it's always interesting. And I get a good salary now, around £12,000 a year. £15,000

Now use this information to complete this form:

Name	Job	Started work	Salary	Job satisfaction*
Ron Lock	van driver	1986 91	£10,000.- a year	+
Pat Jenkins	personnel manager	1980	£15,000.- a year	++

* use the rating system: ++/+/–/– –

2 Working for Metrostar

Write about these three Metrostar workers:

Jenny Lynn	Typist	1981	£7,500	+
Roger Reid	Engineer	1979	£15,000	++
Bill Wyman	Office clerk	1982	£4,000	– –

1 My name is Jenny Lynn. I've been a ¹ _typist_ for ² _seven 12_ years. I quite ³ _like_ my job, and my ⁴ _salary_ is quite ⁵ _good_.

2 I've ⁶ _been working_ as an ⁷ _engineer_ for the company for ⁸ _quite 14_ years, ⁹ _since_ 1979, in fact. I ¹⁰ _love_ my work and my salary is very good.

3 I ¹¹ _hate_ my job. It's very boring and it ¹² _isn't_ well paid. I've worked here for ¹³ _seven six 11_ ¹⁴ _years_, but I'm ¹⁵ _going_ to leave next week!

Unit Four

3 Find the jobs

Complete these words. They are all names of jobs mentioned in Unit Four.

1. C L E R K
2. S T E W A R D E S S
3. P O R T E R *not in it*
4. D O C T O R
5. P O L I C E M A N
6. T E A C H E R
7. M E C H A N I C

4 What should I do?

Sylvia and Larry are talking.

Now look at the rest of their conversation. Larry's responses have been mixed up. Can you match them to what Sylvia says?

1. It's always raining here. *I've been working*
2. I've worked here too long.
3. I always feel tired.
4. I'd love to go to France.
5. But I can't speak French.

a. You should take a holiday.
b. Then you should go there.
c. You should buy an umbrella.
d. You should learn it then.
e. Then you should change your job.

1 c   2 _____   3 _____   4 _____   5 _____

12

Unit Four

5 Read about Clive

Look at this question: *Why is today important for Clive?*
Now read this paragraph:

Today is an important day for Clive Peters. He is driving up to London. He's going to have lunch with his friend, Barbara, and then he's got an interview for a job with Metrostar. Clive has studied Art and Design at Brighton for the last three years and now he has applied for a job as a designer.

Now write in the missing words:

Today is an important day for Clive because he's got an _interview_ for a _job_ as a _designer_ with _Metrostar_.

Read the rest of the passage:

Clive meets Barbara at her flat and they go out for lunch. 'I'm worried about this afternoon,' he tells her.
  'What do you think I should wear for the interview? A suit and tie?'
  Barbara laughs. 'Designers don't wear suits,' she says. 'You should wear a nice shirt and sweater. And wear that brown jacket. It always looks nice.'
  'I'd really like to get this job,' says Clive.
  'Metrostar are a good company to work for. They pay good money too.'
  'Don't worry about it,' says Barbara. 'Just tell them about yourself and show them your work. Then you'll get the job.'

Mark these statements right (√) or wrong (×):

1 Clive is driving to London with Barbara.   ×
2 He's got an interview with Metrostar today.   √
3 He thinks he should wear a suit for the interview.   √
4 Barbara thinks so too.   ×
5 Clive would like to work for Metrostar.   √
6 They pay good salaries.   √
7 Clive is worried about the interview.   √
8 Barbara doesn't think he'll get the job.   ×

Unit Five

1 Comparisons

Look at some of the people in the 'Personality of the Year' contest again:

Bruce Bantock
AGE 27
HEIGHT 178 cm
WEIGHT 73 kg

Steve Shallow
AGE 26
HEIGHT 193 cm
WEIGHT 79 kg

Terry Tong
AGE 25
HEIGHT 182 cm
WEIGHT 75 kg

Now look at these statements:

Bruce is older than Steve.
He's older than Terry too.
Bruce is the oldest of the three.

Now write three similar sentences comparing the height of the three men. (You will need to start with Steve this time.)

1. Steve is taller than Terry.
2. He's taller than Bruce, too.
3. Steve is the tallest of the three.

Now write three more sentences comparing their weights.

4. Steve is heavier than Terry.
5. He's heavier than Bruce, too.
6. Steve is the heaviest of the three.

2 Missing words

Write in the missing words. Choose from the words in this box: | at in on to of

I went ¹ _to_ town to buy a new watch. There's a good shop ² _in_ the centre ³ _of_ town, ⁴ _at_ the corner ⁵ _of_ Market Street and King's Row. I looked ⁶ _at_ the watches ⁷ _in_ the window ⁸ _of_ the shop yesterday.

Unit Five

3 Long, longer, longest

Look at this table of the world's longest rivers:

River	Country	Length (km)
Nile	Sudan Egypt	6,670
Amazon	Brazil	6,448
Mississippi	USA	5,970

Now write about them:

1 The _Nile_ is the _longest_ river in the world.
2 The longest _river_ in _Brazil_ ~~the world~~ is the Amazon.
3 The Nile and the _Amazon_ are both _longer_ than the Mississippi.
4 The _Nile_ is about 200 kilometres _longer_ than the _Amazon_.
5 The _Mississippi_ is the third _longest_ river in the world.

4 And or but?

Look:

> This book is very long.   → This book is very long *and* it's
> It's very boring too.   very boring too.
>
> This book is very long.   → This book is very long *but*
> It's very interesting.   it's very interesting.

Should you use *and* or *but* to join these sentences?

1 Electromart is a big shop.
  It sells a lot of radios.
  and ✓   but ____

2 Sellbury's sell radios too.
  They are more expensive.
  and ____   but ✓

3 I know another shop.
  It's the cheapest of the three.
  and ✓   but ____

4 It's called Discount 85.
  I always go there.
  and ✓   but ____

5 It's only a small shop.
  Its radios are the cheapest.
  and ____   but ✓

5 Your shops

Now write about three shops in your town.

Unit Five

6 Which shop is cheapest?

Read this passage:

Claire Walton looked at food prices in three shops and compared them. The three shops were Bexco, JRV, and Martin's. She found out what they charged for three things – sugar, tea, and cornflakes. Here's what she found.

'The cheapest shop of the three was JRV. They charged 50p for sugar, but only 45p for tea and 70p for cornflakes. The next cheapest was Martin's. There I paid 49p for sugar, but 50p for tea and 75p for cornflakes. The most expensive shop was Bexco. It's a very big shop and it had the highest prices. It cost me 52p for sugar, 49p for tea, and 79p for cornflakes. Quite a difference!'

This table shows Claire's findings. Fill in the gaps.

	Sugar	_Tea_	Cornflakes
Bexco	52p	49p	79p
JRV	50p	45p	70p
Martin's	49p	50p	75p

7 Connections

Look at the reading passage again. What do these words mean?

1 ... and compared *them*   them = food prices

2 *She* found out ...   She = Claire Walton.

3 ... what *they* charged   they = the shops

4 There *I* paid ...   I = Claire Walton

5 *It's* a very big shop ...   It = Bexco

Unit Six

1 City, town or village?

Look at these sentences: ***Edinburgh is big. Its population is 400,000. It's a city.***
Now look at these descriptions of other places in Britain. Complete them, using either *city*, *town* or *village*.

1 Lancaster is smaller than Edinburgh. Its population is 50,000. It's a ___town___.
2 Ashdon is very small. Only 400 people live there. It's a ___village___.
3 Harlow is a ___town___. About 70,000 people live there.
4 Birmingham is a big ___city___. It has a population of a million people.
5 Castley is very beautiful. It's a small ___village___ in the west of England. Only about 600 people live there.

2 Describe these places

Look at this table:

Reading	town	100,000	south
Hornby	village	900	north
Bristol	city	300,000	west
Brighton	town	100,000	south
Colchester	town	60,000	east
Coventry	city	400,000	centre
Hawkchurch	village	431	south-west

Now read this description:
Reading is a town. Its population is 100,000. It's in the south of England.

Write similar sentences about the other places in the table.

3 Write about you

Now write about yourself:

I live in _____. It's a _____. It has a population of _____. It's in the _____ of _____.

Unit Six

4 Can you read it?

Claire is in Paris for a week. She sends a postcard to her friend, Mike. Look:

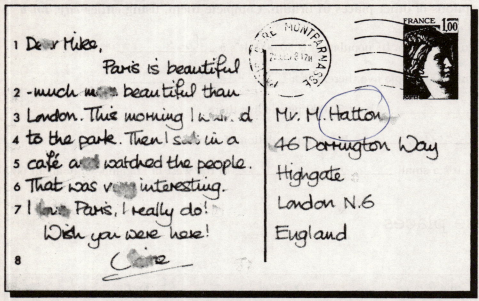

Mike couldn't read the postcard very well because it got wet and some of the words weren't clear. Can you help him by writing in the missing words?

1 _Dear_ 2 _more_ 3 _went_
4 _sat_   5 _and_   6 _very_
7 _love_ 8 _Claire_

5 Crossword

Across
1 I'd like to live in a _____ like Bristol.
4 How _____ cinemas are there in your town?
7 Dave wants to live in a _____ in London.
8 Bristol isn't _____ big as London.

Down
2 Are villages more friendly _____ towns?
3 Villages are too _____: I prefer cities.
5 Cities can be very lonely places _____ first.
6 But I've lived in London for _____, and I love it!

Unit Six

6 Talking to an artist

Bernard Wheaton, an artist, lives in Castley. Claire Walton talks to him about it.

CLAIRE: How long have you been living here in Castley?
BERNARD: About three years.
CLAIRE: And what do you think of it?
BERNARD: I like it. I like living here very much. It's a small place and very, very quiet. But the people are friendly.
CLAIRE: Have you always lived in a village?
BERNARD: No, no. In fact, I was born in Manchester and I went to school there. But I hated it.
CLAIRE: You hated Manchester? Why?
BERNARD: It was too big and too dirty. Of course, it's changed a lot since then. There isn't as much industry there now. But I still prefer living in a village like Castley.
CLAIRE: Isn't it very quiet there?
BERNARD: Yes, I suppose it is. But I don't mind that. I like quiet. I need quiet for my work. I'd really like to live right out in the country. In fact, I'm looking for a cottage at the moment.
CLAIRE: What do you do in your free time? Is there much to do in Castley?
BERNARD: Well, there aren't a lot of discos and night-clubs! No, I suppose there isn't much to do in Castley. When I finish painting, I usually go for a walk along the river. It's lovely there. Then I go into the village pub to have a drink and meet my friends.
CLAIRE: Will you be sorry to leave Castley?
BERNARD: In a way, I will [shall]. I've enjoyed living here.

Now mark these statements right (√) or wrong (×).

1 Bernard has been living in Castley for about three years.   √
2 Castley is a small town.   ×
3 Bernard doesn't like the people in Castley.   ×
4 Bernard lived in Manchester before he lived in a village.   √
5 He prefers living in Manchester to living in Castley.   ×
6 There's less industry in Manchester now.   √
7 He likes Castley because it's quiet.   √
8 Bernard likes going for walks.   √

7 Where you live

Now write about where you live. Do you like it? Why? Are there any things you don't like about it? What are they?

Unit Seven

1 The weather   ☁ = cloudy   🌧 = rainy   ☀ = sunny

Read what the weatherman says about the weather in England. Then tick the picture he is talking about.

1 'Today has been cloudy over most of the country, but there has been some rain in the south.'

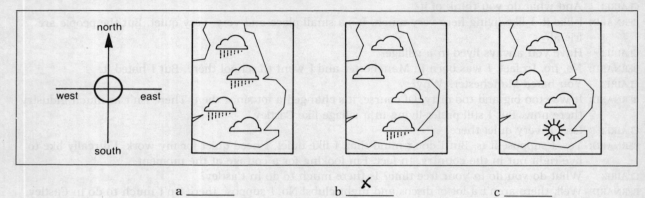

a _____   b ✗ _____   c _____

2 'Tomorrow it will be sunny in the south and west. There will be some rain in the north. The rest of the country will be cloudy.'

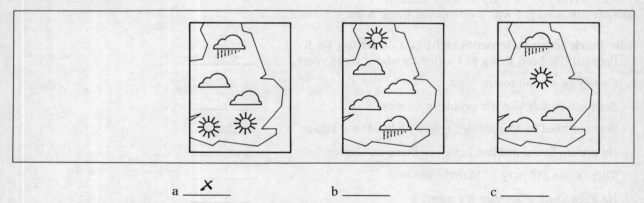

a ✗ _____   b _____   c _____

3 'The day after tomorrow will be cloudy in the south, with some rain in the south-east. Most of the rest of the country will be sunny, but there will be some rain in the north.'

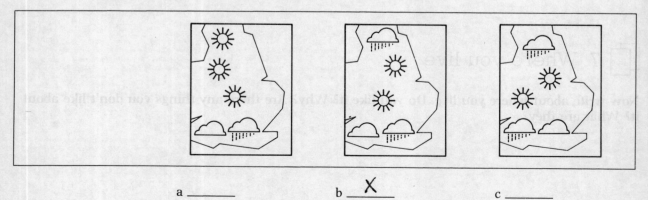

a _____   b ✗ _____   c _____

Unit Seven

2 Since, for or ago?

> It's cold today.
> It's been cold for four days.
> It's been cold since Tuesday.
> It rained two days ago.

Complete these sentences using either *since*, *for* or *ago*:

1 David left home ten years __ago__.
2 He hasn't been back __since__ then.
3 He lived in Mexico __for__ two years.
4 Then he lived in America __for__ seven years.
5 He's been in England __since__ January.
6 He saw his wife half an hour __ago__.

3 Expressions

Complete the expressions in these sentences. Use the following words:

> ~~good~~ ~~free~~ ~~from~~ ~~like~~
> ~~first~~ ~~way~~ ~~that~~ ~~for~~

1 John is very busy: he has very little __free__ time.
2 Judy said it was love at __first__ sight.
3 Bernard is a good gardener. He's very __good__ with his hands.
4 John's car sank __like__ a stone.
5 Better weather is on the __way__ tomorrow.
6 There are no cinemas or things like __that__ in Killbrae.
7 You'll hear __from__ me in a few days.
8 I'm afraid that's all we have time __for__ now.

Unit Seven

4 Jigsaw reading

This is a letter from a woman called Nancy to her friend in Venezuela, Carlos. Finish the parts on the left (1–9) with the parts on the right (a–i).

1. h   2. e   3. a   4. i   5. b   6. d   7. c   8. g   9. f

Dear Carlos,

1. It has been a long time since I last heard from you. I hope
2. I have been very busy the past few months. As I think I told you in my last letter, I am
3. The weather here has been terrible! Perhaps you have read about it in your newspapers. It started
4. The snow was so
5. It was worst of all in Scotland. The weather there is usually colder
6. But even here in southern England, the temperature fell to below
7. In some parts of the country, a few people even froze
8. You don't know how lucky you are to live in a country
9. In your last letter you said you wanted to spend a year in England. Well, if you

a) snowing a week ago and it hasn't stopped since.
b) than it is here in southern England.
c) to death in their cars and a lot of animals on farms died, too.
d) freezing point several days ago.
e) going to take some important exams soon, so I have been studying a lot.
f) do, be sure to bring lots of warm clothing with you!
g) where it never snows and the weather is usually warm!
h) everything is all right and that you are well.
i) heavy in some places that the traffic on the roads couldn't move and all the trains stopped.

That's all for now. Hope to hear from you soon!
Yours,
Nancy

 Now write the letter out in full. Put it into three or four separate paragraphs.

Unit Eight

1 Getting there

Eric Cook is talking about getting to work.

"I go to work by car. It usually takes me about forty minutes."

Now look at what these people say about travelling. Complete the table in the same way as for Eric.

Jill: "Last year I went to the south of France by train. It took a long time — almost ten hours!"

Arnold: "I walk to work every day. It only takes me ten minutes. I don't need a car."

Eileen: "I flew to New York last year. It took me only seven hours."

Claire: "Sometimes I drive my car to work and sometimes I cycle. If I go by car, it takes me twenty minutes. If I cycle, it takes me an hour. But I prefer cycling."

	🚶	🚲	🚗	🚆	✈
Jill				10 hours	
Arnold	10 mins				
Eileen					7 hours
Claire		1 hour	20 mins		

2 Write about yourself

How do you usually come to work? How long does it take you? If you have travelled recently, where did you go, how did you travel and how long did it take you?

Unit Eight

3 Claire's trip

Claire is talking about her trip to the United States. Complete these sentences, choosing from the words listed after each one:

1 Last year I went to America ____on____ business. a at (b) on c in

2 This year I'm going to ____take____ a holiday. *but: go on holiday.* (a) take b go c make

3 I'm going to visit my uncle ____for____ a few days. a since (b) for c at

4 He's lived in San Francisco ____since____ 1967. a till b for (c) since

5 I'm flying to New York, ____then____ I'm taking the train to San Francisco. a because (b) then c since

4 Fix these sentences

The following sentences have been broken into two halves. Can you put them together again correctly?

1 If you go on foot,   a) it won't cost very much.
2 If you take the fast train, b) I'll tell you how to get there.
3 If you go by bus,   c) it'll take you more than an hour.
4 If you visit London,   d) you'll be there on time.
5 If you ask me tomorrow,   e) you can stay with my friend.

1__c__ 2_____ 3_____ 4_____ 5_____

5 Giving directions

Tell someone how to get from your home to a place of interest in your town. There is more than one way to get there: *If you go by bus . . .; if you go by car . . .; if you walk . . .*

Unit Eight

6 Role play

You are a travel agent. Look at this airline timetable and answer the questions which customers ask you.

Pan Am's Transatlantic Flights from London				
		dep.	arr.	
NEW YORK	PA 101	11.00	13.35	
DETROIT	PA 101	11.00	17.20	*1
MIAMI	PA 99	11.15	15.45	
SEATTLE	PA 125	12.45	14.25	*2
WASHINGTON DC	PA 103	11.30	17.25	*3
*except 1 Mon/Tues 2 Fri/Sat 3 Tues/Thurs				

1 Is there a flight to New York this morning?

Yes, there's ~~one at~~ 11 o'clock.

2 When does it leave?

It leaves at 11.00 a.m.

3 What's the number of the Seattle flight, please?

PA 125

4 Can I fly there next Sunday?

Yes, you can.

5 If I take flight PA 99, what time will I get into Miami?

15.45

25

Unit Nine

1 Why I had to sell

United Football Club have just sold one of their players, Joe Hacker, for £1,000,000. Claire Walton talks to United's manager, Ron Mangold, about it.

CLAIRE: Ron, last year you called Joe Hacker 'United's best player'.
RON: That's right. And he's still a great player.
CLAIRE: But now you've sold him. Why?
RON: The answer is simple: money. We had to sell him. We couldn't afford to keep him. When Rovers offered us a million pounds for Joe, we had to take it.
CLAIRE: Was Joe unhappy at United? Did he want to leave?
RON: No, he didn't want to leave. But Rovers can pay him much more than we could. They've got the money. They can afford it. But we can't.
CLAIRE: What do the United fans think about Joe's transfer? Are they pleased?
RON: No, of course they're not. But we've still got a good team this year – even without Joe. I hope the fans will still come and watch us play.
CLAIRE: Ron, one final question. A million pounds is a lot of money. What are you going to do with it? Do you plan to buy new players?
RON: No, we plan to build a bigger and better club. We're going to build a new stadium here which will be the best in the country. And that's only the start. Years ago, United was one of the top clubs in the country. Now we want it to be one of the top clubs again.
CLAIRE: Ron Mangold, thank you for talking to me.

Now mark these statements right (√) or wrong (×):

1 Joe Hacker is a great player.   √
2 Joe wasn't happy at United.   ×
3 United sold Joe because they needed the money.   √
4 Rovers are richer than United.   √
5 United's fans are unhappy about Joe's transfer.   √
6 United are going to buy new players.   ×
7 United is one of the country's top clubs.   ×
8 Its new stadium will be the (biggest) in the country.   best   ×

Unit Nine

2 Connections

Look at Claire's interview again. What do these words mean?

1. But now you've sold *him*.   him = _Joe Hacker_
2. ... we had to take *it*.   it = _A million pounds (the sum of)_
3. *They* can afford it.   they = _Rovers._
4. But *we* can't.   we = _United_
5. Are *they* pleased?   they = _the fans_
6. Now we want *it* to be ...   it = _United_

3 Reporting

The *Daily News* reported Claire's interview with Ron Mangold. Read it and write in the missing words:

Daily News

United lose Joe Hacker to Rovers

In an ___interview___ with Claire Walton yesterday, United's ¹___manager___, Ron Mangold, explained why he had to ²___sell___ Joe Hacker, United's star player. 'We needed the money,' ³___Ron/he___ said. Mangold went on to say that United were ⁴___still___ a good team. He ⁵___hoped___ United's fans would still come and watch the team this year. He said he was ⁶___not___ going to buy new players. 'We're ⁷___planning (going)___ to build a new stadium,' Mangold declared. 'It will be the ⁸___best___ in the country.'

Unit Nine

4 Match the headlines

Which story goes with which headline? Can you match them?

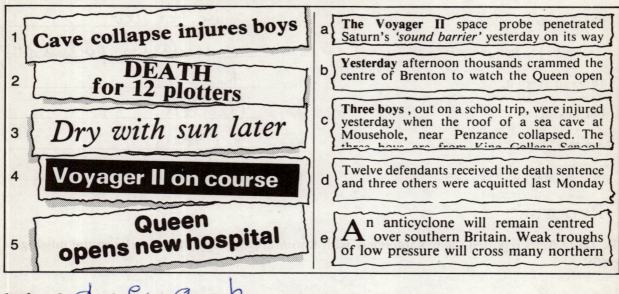

1 _c_ 2 _d_ 3 _e_ 4 _a_ 5 _b_

5 Who or which?

Use *who* or *which* to join these sentences:

1. Claire wanted to speak to Joe Hacker.
   He plays for Rovers now.

   Claire wanted to speak to Joe Hacker, who plays for Rovers now.

2. Last year he played for United. _which_
   ~~It~~ is a very good club.

3. Joe scored 35 goals last year. _which_
   ~~That~~ is a record.

4. Joe will enjoy playing with Bobby King. _who_
   ~~Bobby~~ is the captain of Rovers.

Kernel Two Answer key

Note: an asterisk (*) beside an exercise number indicates where variations on the answers given are possible.

Unit One

Ex 1 1 ... beat ... five ... 2 ... walked out ... 3 ... police ... people ... 4 ... won ... tenth ...
Ex 2 C
Ex 3 1 curly 2 bald 3 dark/short 4 long/straight
Ex 4 B
Ex 6 1 × 2 ✓ 3 ✓ 4 ✓ 5 × 6 ×

Unit Two

Ex 1 Bill: + + − − −
          Joy: − + ++ ++
Alex loves reading books, but he hates watching television. He quite likes going for walks, but he doesn't like listening to music.
Ex 3 1 Would you like to come outside? 2 Would you like to have a seat? 3 Would you like to have a drink? 4 Would you like to play tennis on Sunday? 5 Would you like to go for a walk tomorrow?
Ex 4 *Across* 2 walks 3 hobby 6 television *Down* 1 play 3 hate 4 ball 5 music
Ex 5 1 ✓ 2 ✓ 3 × 4 ✓ 5 × 6 × 7 × 8 ✓
Ex 6 1 interested 2 long 3 film 4 How 5 much 6 cost 7 What 8 do

Unit Three

Ex 1 2 happiest 3 handsomest/most handsome 4 most attractive 5 happier 6 more difficult 7 better
Ex 2 1 A 2 C 3 A 4 B
Ex 3 2 Shut the door, please. 3 Would you come over here, please? 3 Sit down, please. 5 Would you tell me your name, please? 6 Read these letters on the wall, please. 7 Would you stop reading now, please? 8 Close your eyes, please.
Ex 4 c
Ex 5* 2 Then I'm going to phone Eric. 3 At eleven o'clock I've got a *News in Focus* meeting. 4 Then at half-past twelve I'm having lunch with Judith. 5 In the evening I've got a yoga class. 6 Then I'm going to watch *Casablanca* on television.

Unit Four

Ex 1

Name	Job	Started work	Salary	Job satisfaction
Ron Lock	Van driver	(this year minus 2)	£8,000	+
Pat Jenkins	Personnel manager	1980	£12,000	++

Ex 2 1 typist 2 (present year − 1981) 3 like 4 salary 5 good 6 worked 7 engineer 8 (present year − 1979) 9 since 10 love 11 hate 12 isn't 13 (present year − 1982) 14 year(s) 15 going
Ex 3 1 clerk 2 stewardess 3 porter 4 doctor 5 policeman 6 teacher 7 mechanic
Ex 4 2 e 3 a 4 b 5 d
Ex 5 Today is an important day for Clive because he's got an interview for a job as a designer with Metrostar.
1 × 2 ✓ 3 ✓ 4 × 5 ✓ 6 ✓ 7 ✓ 8 ×

Unit Five

Ex 1 1 Steve is taller than Terry/Bruce. 2 He's taller than Bruce/Terry too. 3 Steve is the tallest of the three. 4 Steve is heavier than Terry/Bruce. 5 He's heavier than Bruce/Terry too. 6 Steve is the heaviest of the three.
Ex 2 1 to 2 in 3 of 4 at 5 of 6 at 7 in 8 of
Ex 3 2 The longest river in Brazil is the Amazon. 3 The Nile and the Amazon are both longer than the Mississippi. 4 The Amazon is about 200 kilometres shorter than the Nile. 5 The Mississippi is the third longest river in the world.
Ex 4 2 but 3 and 4 and 5 but
Ex 6

Shop	Sugar	Tea	Cornflakes
Bexco	**52p**	49p	79p
JRV	50p	45p	**70p**
Martin's	49p	50p	75p

Ex 7 1 food prices 2 Claire Walton 3 the (three) shops 4 Claire Walton 5 Bexco

Unit Six

Ex 1 1 town 2 village 3 town 4 city 5 village
Ex 2 Hornby is a village. Its population is 900. It's in the north of England.
Bristol is a city. Its population is 300,000. It's in the west of England.
Brighton is a town. Its population is 100,000. It's in the south of England.
Colchester is a town. Its population is 60,000. It's in the east of England.
Coventry is a city. Its population is 400,000. It's in the centre of England.
Hawkchurch is a village. Its population is 431. It's in the south-west of England.
Ex 4 2 more 3 walked 4 sat 5 and 6 very 7 love 8 Claire
Ex 5 *Across* 1 city 4 many 7 flat 8 as *Down* 2 than 3 small 5 at 6 years
Ex 6 1 √ 2 × 3 × 4 √ 5 × 6 √ 7 √ 8 √

Unit Seven

Ex 1 1 b 2 a 3 b
Ex 2 1 ago 2 since 3 for 4 for 5 since 6 ago
Ex 3 2 first 3 good 4 like 5 way 6 that 7 from 8 for
Ex 4 1 h 2 e 3 a 4 i 5 b 6 d 7 c 8 g 9 f

Unit Eight

Ex 1

	🚶	🚲	🚗	🚆	✈️
Jill				10 hours	
Arnold	10 minutes				
Eileen					7 hours
Claire		1 hour	20 minutes		

Ex 3 1 on 2 take 3 for 4 since 5 then
Ex 4 2 d 3 a 4 e 5 b
Ex 6 1 Yes, there is. 2 (It leaves) At eleven o'clock. 3 PA 125. 4 Yes, you can. 5 15.45./At a quarter to four (in the afternoon).

Unit Nine

Ex 1 1 √ 2 × 3 √ 4 √ 5 √ 6 × 7 × 8 ×
Ex 2 1 Joe Hacker 2 a million pounds 3 Rovers 4 United 5 the United fans 6 United
Ex 3 1 manager 2 sell 3 he 4 still 5 hoped 6 not 7 going 8 best
Ex 4 2 d 3 e 4 a 5 b
Ex 5 2 Last year he played for United, which is a very good club. 3 Joe scored 35 goals last year, which is a record. 4 Joe will enjoy playing with Bobby King, who is the captain of Rovers.

Unit Ten

Ex 1 1 Can 2 wonder 3 Is 4 Can/Could 5 tell 6 got 7 what/how
Ex 2 3: 2: 4: 5: 6: 1: 7
Ex 3 *Across* 1 steak 4 smells 7 tea 8 weren't *Down* 2 taste 3 raw 5 menu 6 eat
Ex 4 1 Can you tell me where it is? 2 Do you know how I can get there? 3 Can you tell me which bus we take?
Ex 5 1 √ 2 √ 3 × 4 √ 5 × 6 √ 7 × 8 × 9 √ 10 √

Unit Eleven

Ex 1 1 ... saved ... emergency ... at ...
2 ... were ... beaten by ... 'Super Spurs'.
3 ... woman ... was injured ... in ... by ...
4 ... picture ... was ... Police ... arrested ...
Ex 2 c
Ex 3
1 I think we should ... 2 Why don't we ...
3 Let's ... 4 we should ... 5 why don't we ...
6 let's
Ex 4 1 five 2 Most 3 we should 4 pay 5 build 6 improve 7 should

Unit Twelve

Ex 1 2 I used to walk to work, but now I go by car.
3 I used to read books, but now I watch television.
4 I used to drink wine, but now I drink whisky.
5 I used to play football, but now I play darts.
Ex 2 1 Q: When did you start going by car? A: I started going by car last year.
2 Q: When did you start watching television? A: I started watching television a few years ago.
3 Q: When did you start drinking whisky? A: I started drinking whisky just this year.
4 Q: When did you start playing darts? A: I started playing darts about six months ago.
Ex 3* 1 I used to like smoking, but now I can't stand it. 2 I used to love drinking whisky, but now I dislike it. 3 I used to hate taking exercise, but now I enjoy it. 4 I never used to like walking to work, but now I enjoy it. 5 I used to dislike eating fruit, but now I love it.
Ex 5 1 f 2 k 3 c 4 o 5 m 6 h 7 a 8 d 9 p 10 l 11 i 12 e 13 n 14 b 15 g 16 j
Ex 6* 1 walked at least five miles every day 2 eaten very simply 3 got up early 4 smoked 5 worried about anything 6 been married

Unit Thirteen

Ex 1 1 slowly 2 quickly 3 calm 4 dangerous 5 quiet 6 heavily
Ex 2 1 agree 2 disagree 3 agree 4 disagree 5 disagree
Ex 3 1 ✓ 2 ✓ 3 ✗ 4 ✗ 5 ✓ 6 ✓ 7 ✗ 8 ✗
Ex 4 1a Claire agrees with Bob that stones were thrown at the police. b Claire agrees with Sue that a lot of demonstrators were injured by the police.
2* People, like Bob, who support the police against demonstrators.
Ex 5 2 you 3 Yes 4 start 5 ago 6 well

Unit Fourteen

Ex 1 2 I'm afraid they'll ask me questions I can't answer.
3 I hope I like the interviewer.
4 I'm afraid it won't be a popular programme.
5 I hope they give me a drink afterwards.
7 I hope Bill doesn't drink too much.
8 I'm afraid there won't be enough food.
9 I hope Sue brings her cassettes.
10 I hope everyone enjoys the party.
Ex 2 2 f 3 b 4 a 5 d 6 c
Ex 3 2 g 3 d 4 a 5 h 6 b 7 f 8 c
Ex 4* Dear Pat,
I'm worried about Jim. I'm afraid he's working too hard. I must phone him tomorrow. I hope the Birmingham trip is a success. I must cook a special dinner for him on Friday – that's Jim's birthday.
Yours, Edith

Unit Fifteen

Ex 1 2 was waiting 3 was eating . . . heard 4 opened . . . was standing 5 use . . . has broken down
Ex 2 2 Well, I don't. 3 Well, I do. 4 Well, I don't. 5 Well, I do.
Ex 3 1 storm 2 change 3 fool 4 top
Ex 4 You mustn't (must never) go on if the weather's bad. You really mustn't.
You must (always) wear warm clothes. You really must.
You must (always) carry a map and know how to use it. You really must.
You must (always) take extra food with you. You really must.
You must (always) tell someone where you are going. You really must.
Ex 6 1 ✓ 2 ✗ 3 ✗ 4 ✓ 5 ✗ 6 ✓ 7 ✓ 8 ✗
9* Because he didn't take enough care and he was almost killed.

Unit Sixteen

Ex 1 3 I'm sorry I forgot to bring my records.
4 I'm sorry I dropped that green cup. 5 It's a pity it broke. 6 It's a pity your husband was angry with me. 7 I'm sorry I have to go now.
Ex 2 2 You're right. I should have gone for help.
3 You're right. I should have helped the little boy.
4 You're right. I should have called the police.
5 You're right. I should have told them about the fight.
Ex 3 *Across* 1 married 4 soldier 5 loved
Down 2 war 3 killed 6 more

Ex 4 2 Has he? 3 No, I didn't. 4 No, I don't.
5 No, I won't.
Ex 5 1 × 2 √ 3 √ 4 × 5 √ 6 √ 7 ×
8 √ 9 × 10 √

Unit Seventeen

Ex 2 2/a If I were you, I wouldn't buy that dress.
3/e If I were a film star, I'd live in Hollywood.
4/b If I had to live in another country, I'd choose Australia.
5/c If I stopped work, I'd be bored.
Ex 3 b 4 c 1 d 6
Ex 4 2 started teaching 3 working 4 to be
5 I'm not enjoying 6 getting up 7 stopping
Ex 5 2 d 3 h 4 a 5 j 6 f 7 i 8 c
9 g 10 e

Unit Ten

1 Ask the questions

Tony and Helen are in Annie's Bistro. Read their conversation with the waitress and complete the questions.

WAITER: Good evening. ¹_____Can/Could_____ I take your order now?

TONY: Good evening. I'm not sure what to order. I ²_____wonder_____ if you can suggest anything?

WAITER: Well, the Boston Chowder is very good.

HELEN: Chowder? ³_____Is_____ that an American dish?

WAITER: Yes, it is. It's a kind of fish soup.

TONY: Oh, fish soup. ⁴_____Can/Could_____ you ⁵_____tell_____ me if it's got clams or oysters in it? *Venusmuscheln u. Jongele*

WAITER: Yes, it's ⁶_____got_____ lots of oysters.

TONY: Oh dear. Then I'm afraid I can't have it. I can't eat oysters.

HELEN: But *I* love oysters. I'll have the Boston Chowder, please.

WAITER: Thank you. One Boston Chowder. Now ⁷_____What/how_____ about you, sir?

TONY: I'd like to start with a green salad, please.

2 Unmix the recipe

Here is a recipe for making an omelette. The sentences are in the wrong order. Can you find the right order?

6 1 Pour the egg mixture over the potatoes and onions.
2 2 First heat the oil in a frying pan.
1 3 For this recipe you need four eggs, an onion, a large potato and some oil.
3 4 Then chop up the onion and potato and fry them in the hot oil.
4 5 Turn the heat up and cook them for about five minutes.
5 6 When the vegetables are brown, mix the eggs together.
7 7 Turn the omelette out onto a hot plate and serve with a green salad.

_3_ ___ ___ ___ ___ ___ ___

Unit Ten

3 Crossword

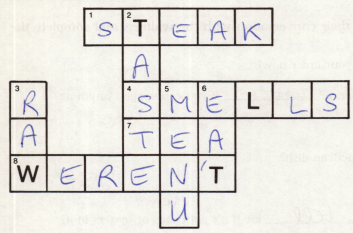

Across
1 Yesterday I ordered a _steak_ in a restaurant. 'I'd like it well done' I said to the waiter.
4 'That _smells_ good,' my wife said when it came.
7 I wanted a cup of _tea_, but they only had coffee.
8 Our friends ordered fish, but they _weren't_ very pleased with it.

Down
2 'This fish doesn't _taste_ very nice,' they said.
3 'They haven't cooked it enough,' I said. 'It looks _raw_ to me.'
5 'You should send it back,' said my wife. 'Choose something else from the _menu_.'
6 'That's right,' I said. 'You shouldn't _eat_ that fish if it doesn't taste all right.'

4 Asking questions

Helen's friend, Jane, wants to go to Annie's Bistro. She asks Helen about it.

Treat the rest of Jane's questions in the same way:

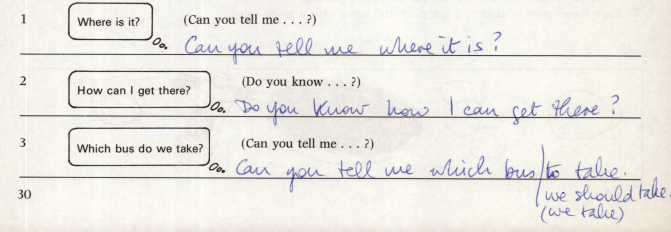

1 Where is it? (Can you tell me . . . ?)
   Can you tell me where it is?

2 How can I get there? (Do you know . . . ?)
   Do you know how I can get there?

3 Which bus do we take? (Can you tell me . . . ?)
   Can you tell me which bus to take. / we should take (we take)

Unit Ten

5 My favourite restaurants

George Bromley writes about restaurants every week in the *Daily Echo*. His article this week is about English food and where to find it.

The George Bromley Column

Visitors to England often ask me where they can find good English food. I usually tell them not to go to traditional English restaurants, especially those where the waiters are dressed up in silly clothes. The prices in these places are always high and the food is usually awful. They should be avoided. It's much better to eat in an English home, if you can. That's where the best English food is cooked. But if you can't do that, there are now two London restaurants that serve good simple English food at reasonable prices.

The first is the *White Hart*, an old pub in Islington. They give you excellent roast beef, served with lightly-cooked fresh vegetables. Their puddings aren't very exciting, so it's best to follow your roast beef with some of their splendid English cheeses. If you drink beer instead of wine, your meal should only cost about £7.50.

My second discovery is *Brook's*, a new restaurant in Chelsea. This is more expensive than the *White Hart*, but it's worth the extra money. Their specialities are steak and chops. They also have a good selection of delicious English puddings. The service is excellent – the staff are courteous and efficient. With a bottle of wine, you'll probably have to pay about £10 a head, but you will have a meal to remember, a meal to remind you that English food *can* be the best in the world. Good eating!

George Bromley

Now mark these statements right (√) or wrong (×):

1 Visitors to England want to eat English food.   √
2 English people eat well at home.   √
3 English restaurants are usually cheap.   ×
4 The food doesn't usually taste very good in English restaurants.   √
5 The *White Hart* is in Yorkshire.   ×
6 You should try the cheese at the *White Hart*.   √
7 *Brook's* is cheaper than the *White Hart*.   ×
8 Roast beef is one of their specialities.   ×
9 *Brook's* have very nice puddings.   √
10 The waiters at *Brook's* are very good.   √

Unit Eleven

1 What happened?

Look at this newspaper headline:

Jewel thieves arrested at airport

Here is the first sentence of the newspaper story:
Yesterday two jewel thieves were arrested at Manchester Airport.

Now look at these headlines. Complete the first sentence of the newspaper story:

1 Transplant man saved by emergency operation

Yesterday George Roebuck, Oxford's transplant man was ___saved___ by an ___emergency___ operation ___at___ St. Margaret's Hospital.

2 UNITED BEATEN BY 'SUPER SPURS'

On Saturday United ___were___ well and truly ___beaten___ ___by___ a Spurs team that deserved the name '___Super Spurs___'.

3 WOMAN INJURED IN BRADFORD BOMB BLAST

A 28-year-old Yorkshire ___woman___, Anne Oddy, ___was___ ___injured___ yesterday ___in___ the centre of Bradford ___by___ a bomb.

4 Police arrest picture slasher

The Royal Institute's most famous ___picture___, Fitter's *Sun and Sand*, ___was___ slashed with a knife yesterday. ___Police___ later ___arrested___ Boris Bolling, an art student.

Unit Eleven

2 Choose the headline

Read this newspaper story, then say which headline you think is best.

> ROCK SINGER BILLY KENNEDY was attacked last night in the El Mogambo night-club in the heart of London's Soho. Billy, lead singer with *The Upbeats*, was asked for his autograph by a fan. An argument started and the police were called. Billy is in hospital with cuts and bruises.

a **Rock star attacks fan in club**

b **Police arrest Kennedy fan**

(c) **Singer attacked in night-club**

d **Night-club owner calls police**

I think headline ___c___ is best.

3 Making suggestions

> Let's / I think we should   do it.
>
> Why don't we   do it?

You are with a friend. Suddenly a man runs up to her and grabs her handbag. Make suggestions about what to do:

A: ___Let's___ run after him.

B: No, he may have a gun. 1 ___I think we should___ tell the police.

A: But then it may be too late. 2 ___Why don't we___ try to catch him now?

B: No, it's too dangerous. There's a police station near here. 3 ___Let's___ go there now and tell them what happened.

A: I still think 4 ___we should___ follow him ourselves.

B: No, 5 ___Why don't we___ leave it to the police?

A: All right. But 6 ___let's___ hurry!

Unit Eleven

4 What's your opinion?

The News in Focus asked viewers for their opinions about how to stop crime. Claire Walton asked people questions like this:

Here are the results of this opinion poll:

	Agree	Disagree	Don't know
1 We should have more policemen.	67%	21%	12%
2 We should pay policemen more money.	33%	47%	20%
3 We should improve prison conditions.	58%	35%	7%
4 We should give criminals longer prison sentences.	72%	20%	8%
5 We should build more prisons.	65%	19%	16%

Now complete this summary of the opinion poll results:

'We asked people ¹___*five*___ questions. The results were very interesting. ²___*Most*___ people thought ³___*we should*___ have more policemen, but only a third thought we should ⁴___*pay*___ them more. Most people thought we should ⁵___*build*___ more prisons and ⁶___*improve*___ conditions in prisons. But the biggest majority thought that criminals ⁷___*should*___ get longer sentences.'

5 Talk to Claire

Claire Walton asks you the questions from the opinion poll. Consider your own country when you answer her questions. Look at Claire's questions in exercise 4 to help you write the dialogue.

Unit Twelve

1 Then and now

Roger Newman is looking at an old photograph of himself:

I used to be thin, but now I'm fat.

Write down more things that Roger said. Use the notes to help you.

1. wear jeans: wear a suit

   I used to wear jeans, but now I wear a suit.

2. walk to work: go by car

   I used to walk to work, but now I go by car.

3. read books: watch television

   I used to read books, but now I watch television.

4. drink wine: drink whisky

   I used to drink wine, but now I drink whisky.

5. play football: play darts

   I used to play football, but now I play darts.

2 You ask Roger

You are asking Roger when he started doing the things he does now:

When did you start wearing a suit?

I started wearing a suit about three years ago.

Here are Roger's answers to the rest of the questions. Write down your questions and Roger's answers in full:

1. go by car – last year *When did you start going by car? I started going by car one year ago.*
2. watch television – a few years ago *When did you start watching TV? I started watching TV a few years ago.*
3. drink whisky – just this year *When did you start drinking whisky? I started drinking whisky just this year.*
4. play darts – about six months ago *When did you start playing darts? I started playing about 6 months ago.*

Unit Twelve

3 James Taylor then and now

James Taylor is Laura Taylor's husband. He talks about what he used to like and what he likes now:

I never used to like cycling, but now I love it.

This table shows how James's likes and dislikes have changed:

	Past	Present
1 smoking	+	−
2 drinking whisky	+	−
3 taking exercise	−	+
4 walking to work	−	+
5 eating fruit	−	+

Write about James's likes and dislikes. Use words like these:

| like | dislike | love |
| hate | enjoy | can't stand |

1 *I used to like smoking, but I dislike it now.*
2 *I used to enjoy drinking whisky but I can't stand it now.*
3 *I never used to take I used to hate taking exercise but I love it now.*
4 *I never used to walk I used to dislike walking to work, but I enjoy it now.*
5 *I never used to eat I used to hate eating fruit, but I love it now.*

4 I used to like it

Now write in the same way about how your own likes and dislikes have changed.

Unit Twelve

5 Jigsaw reading

Read this article. Then finish the incomplete sentences (1–16) with one of the phrases (a–p) below the article.

Secrets of a long and healthy life

Yesterday afternoon in a village near Bristol, a tall old man with a good suntan celebrated his birthday with some friends. After the party he played tennis and then went for a ¹ _five-mile walk_ with some of his guests. There was nothing unusual in this. The man, whose name was Mr Misha Weibold, ² _has been celebrating_ his birthday in this way for a long time. The only unusual thing is that Mr Weibold was ninety-five years old yesterday.

'I don't walk as fast as ³ _I used to_ and my eyes aren't quite as good as ⁴ _they were_, but otherwise I feel just as fit as I was when I was thirty', Mr Weibold later told one of our reporters. Mr Weibold was ⁵ _born in Russia & came_ to this country when he was twenty years old. He ⁶ _has been living_ near Bristol for the last fifty years. When asked what his secret was for such a long and healthy life, he answered, 'There are three things ⁷ _which_ I've always done and three things I've ⁸ _never done_. First of all, I've always walked at least ⁹ _five miles_ every day. ¹⁰ _Secondly_, I've always eaten very simply: things like brown rice and vegetables. Thirdly, I've always been in the habit of ¹¹ _getting up early_: never later than six o'clock in the winter and five o'clock in the summer.

'Then there are the three things ¹² _which I've never done_. I've never ¹³ _smoked_ a cigarette in all my life! I've never ¹⁴ _worried_ about anything. And I've never been married. I've believed that marriage was a very unhealthy thing and now I'm sure of it. When I was sixty, I used to have a lot of friends ¹⁵ _who were married_. And do you know ¹⁶ _what has happened to them_. They're all dead!'

a) ~~which~~ b) ~~worried~~ c) I used to d) ~~never done~~ e) ~~which I've never done~~ f) ~~five-mile walk~~ g) ~~who were married~~ h) has been living i) ~~getting up early~~ j) ~~what has happened to them?~~ k) has been celebrating l) ~~Secondly~~ m) ~~born in Russia and came~~ n) ~~smoked~~ o) ~~they were~~ p) ~~five miles~~

6 Always and never

Write down the three things Mr Weibold has always done (1–3) and the three things he has never done (4–6).

Mr Weibold has always:

1 _walked at least 5 miles a day._
2 _got up at 5 or 6 every morning._
3 _eaten very simply._

Mr Weibold has never:

1 _smoked a cigarette._
2 _got married._
3 _worried._

Unit Thirteen

1 Complete the conversation

Paul and Debbie are driving to a party. Read their conversation and complete it by using these words:

calm	quickly
quiet	slowly
dangerous	heavily

DEBBIE: Drive more ¹ _slowly_ Paul.

PAUL: But I can't. We'll be late for the party. I'm sorry, but I've got to drive ² _quickly_.

DEBBIE: Keep ³ _calm_, Paul. And please slow down. It's ⁴ _dangerous_ to drive like this.

PAUL: Be ⁵ _quiet_, will you? I'm trying to drive.

DEBBIE: Now it's raining. It's raining ⁶ _heavily_. Please be more careful. Look out, Paul! For God's sake, look out!!

2 Agreeing and disagreeing

Are the second speakers in each of these conversations agreeing or disagreeing? Tick the correct answer. For example, if the second speaker is disagreeing: agree_____ disagree__✓__

1. A: The police have a really difficult job.
   B: Yes, that's right.   agree __✓__ disagree_____

2. A: We need nuclear power.
   B: How can you say that?   agree_____ disagree __✓__

3. A: It's dangerous to drive too fast.
   B: That's exactly what I think.   agree __✓__ disagree_____

4. A: *The News in Focus* isn't very interesting tonight.
   B: I don't agree with you at all.   agree_____ disagree __✓__

5. A: Demonstrating against nuclear power is a waste of time.
   B: A waste of time? Nonsense!   agree_____ disagree __✓__

Unit Thirteen

3 Points of view

Claire Walton talked to two people who were at the Helmby riot. One was Bob McEwan, a policeman; the other was Sue Lloyd, a demonstrator. Claire spoke to Bob first:

CLAIRE: A lot of people were hurt in the riot. Who started the trouble, Bob?
BOB: The demonstrators, of course. They were trying to get into the field and we were trying to keep them back. Then some idiots at the back started throwing stones at us.
CLAIRE: Do you agree with that, Sue?
SUE: No, certainly not. Look, I was at the front of the demonstration. The police were pushing us back the whole time. They were pushing really hard. I wasn't hurt, but a boy standing next to me was knocked down. It was really frightening.
CLAIRE: Was that when the demonstrators started throwing stones?
SUE: I didn't see anyone throwing stones.
BOB: Oh, really, that's ridiculous –
SUE: But I did see policemen hitting people and kicking them!
BOB: That's rubbish! Look, there are more than twenty policemen in hospital now. If no one threw stones, how do you explain that?
CLAIRE: Stones *were* thrown at the police. There's no doubt about that, Sue.
SUE: Well, maybe you're right. I just didn't see it. But how do *you* explain the fifty demonstrators in hospital? They're there because the police beat them up!
CLAIRE: A lot of demonstrators *were* injured, Bob.
BOB: Well, of course they were. When policemen are attacked, naturally they'll defend themselves.
SUE: How can you say that? We didn't attack you – you attacked us!
BOB: That's nonsense!
SUE: You people are trying to stop free speech in this country!
BOB: Rubbish! I've never heard such nonsense in my life! The truth is . . .
CLAIRE: I'm sorry, but that's all we have time for today. Bob McEwan, Sue Lloyd, thank you both very much.

Mark these statements right (✓) or wrong (×):

1 Many people were hurt at Helmby. ✓
2 Bob thinks the demonstrators started the trouble. ✓
3 Sue agrees with him. ✗
4 Someone knocked Sue down. ✗
5 Sue agrees that some demonstrators threw stones. ✓
6 The demonstrators in hospital were injured by the police. ✓
7 Bob thinks the police attacked the demonstrators. ✗
8 He agrees that the police are trying to stop free speech. ✗

Unit Thirteen

4 Discuss

Claire Walton agrees with one of Bob's statements and with one of Sue's statements. Write down the statements she agrees with:

1a Claire agrees with Bob that *stones were thrown at the police.*

b Claire agrees with Sue that *a lot of demonstrators were injured by the police.*

What does Sue mean when she talks about 'You people'?

2 *She means people like Bob who support the police against demonstrators.*

5 Word square

Can you find six words in this square and write them in these sentences? The first one is shown for you.

1 Who *stole* the diamonds?

2 Do *you* know?

3 *Yes,* I think I do.

4 When did you *start* playing tennis?

5 I started about six months *ago*.

6 But I'm afraid I don't play very *well*.

Unit Fourteen

1 Hopes and fears

Charles L. Night is going to be interviewed on television. Write down his hopes and fears. Use these notes to help you:

1. I/not late
   I hope I'm not late.

2. they/ask me/questions/can't answer
   I'm afraid they'll ask me questions I can't answer.

3. I/like/the interviewer
   I hope I'll like the interviewer.

4. it/won't be/a popular programme
   I'm afraid it won't be a popular programme.

5. they/give me/a drink afterwards
   I hope they'll give me a drink afterwards.

Lorraine Taylor is planning a party. Write about her hopes and fears in the same way:

6. no one/come
   I'm afraid no one will come.

7. Bill/not drink/too much
   I hope Bill won't drink too much.

8. there/be/not enough/food
   I'm afraid there won't be enough food.

9. Sue/bring/her cassettes
   I hope Sue will bring her cassettes.

10. everyone/enjoy the party
    I hope everyone will enjoy the party.

Unit Fourteen

2 Making an offer

In each of these pictures the speaker is offering to do something. What do you think he/she is saying? Choose from the sentences given below:

a

b

c

d

e

f

1 Would you like me to close the door?   _e_
2 Shall I buy the tickets?   _f_
3 Let me carry your case.   _b_
4 Would you like me to turn the radio down?   _a_
5 Shall I help you with the dishes?   _d_
6 Would you like me to take your coat?   _c_

Unit Fourteen

3 Opposites

Hope and *fear* mean the opposite of each other. Can you arrange the following lists of words into eight pairs of opposites?

1	below	a	sit	1	*below*	*above*
2	play	b	badly	2	*play*	*work*
3	late	c	old	3	*late*	*early*
4	stand	d	early	4	*stand*	*sit*
5	good	e	above	5	*good*	*bad*
6	well	f	start	6	*well*	*badly*
7	stop	g	work	7	*stop*	*start*
8	young	h	bad	8	*young*	*old*

4 Edith's diary

Edith Horton's husband, Jim, is away in Birmingham on business. Edith writes about her feelings in her diary. Read her diary then re-write it in the form of a letter to a friend.

Tuesday 5

Worried about J. Afraid he's working too hard. Must phone him tomorrow. Hope Birmingham trip a success. Must cook special dinner Friday – J's birthday.

5 Silverstone Way
Harrow
Middlesex
5th May

Dear Pat,

I'm worried about Jim. I'm afraid he's working too hard. I must phone him tomorrow. I hope the Birmingham trip is a success. I must cook a special dinner for him on Friday – that's Jim's birthday.

Yours,
Edith

Unit Fifteen

1 A policeman calls

> When the phone *rang*, I *was washing* my car.

Use a form of the verbs in brackets to complete this story:

1 When I (*get up*) this morning, the sun (*shine*).

   got up   _was shining_

2 A police car (*wait*) outside my house.

   was waiting

3 I (*eat*) my breakfast when I (*hear*) a knock at the door.

   I was eating   _heard_

4 When I (*open*) the door, a policeman (*stand*) there.

   I opened   _was standing_

5 'Can I (*use*) your phone?' he said. 'My car (*break down*).'

   Can I use   _has broken down._

2 Arguing

- I don't think we should stop. — Well, I do.
- I think we should go on. — Well, I don't.

Eileen Chase wants to learn a foreign language. Mark, her husband, disagrees. Write down what Mark says against each of Eileen's statements:

1 I think we should learn another language.   _Well, I don't._

2 I think Spanish would be nice.   _Well, I don't._

3 I don't think it would be very difficult.   _Well, I do._

4 I think Spanish is a very useful language.   _Well, I don't._

5 I don't like staying at home every night.   _Well, I do._

Unit Fifteen

3 Scrambles

Here are four scrambled words. Can you unscramble them and write them in these sentences?

| P | T | O |

| G | E | A | N | H | C |

| M | R | O | T | S |

| O | L | O | F |

1 I'm afraid there's going to be a bad ___storm___.
2 Nonsense! The weather isn't going to ___change___ now.
3 Don't be a ___fool___! You must come back.
4 No, I must get to the ___top___ of the mountain!

4 Safety on the mountains

Read these rules about safety on the mountains. They tell you what you must and mustn't do when you walk in the mountains.

Mountain Safety

Enjoy your mountains, but be careful.
When you walk in the mountains in winter follow these simple rules:
NEVER go out alone
NEVER go on if the weather is bad *You mustn't go on if the weather is bad. You really mustn't.*
ALWAYS wear warm clothes *You must always wear warm clothes. You really must.*
ALWAYS carry a map — and know how to use it! *You must always carry a map & know how to use it. You really must.*
ALWAYS take extra food with you *You must always take extra food with you. You really must.*
ALWAYS tell someone where you are going *You must always tell someone where you're going. You really must.*
Always obey these rules and enjoy your mountains in safety.

 Tell David to follow these rules like this:

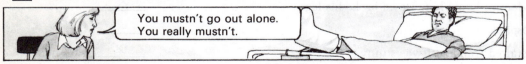

You mustn't go out alone.
You really mustn't.

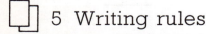 5 Writing rules

Now write the rules for one of the following:
1 swimming in the sea
2 aeroplane passengers landing
3 keeping indoor plants

45

Unit Fifteen

6 Mountain rescue

Jock Douglas is the head of the Mountain Rescue Team. Claire Walton asks him about ~~the rescue of~~ David Gregg. 's rescue!

CLAIRE: Where did you find him?
JOCK: When we found him, he was sheltering under a big rock.
CLAIRE: How was he?
JOCK: He was very cold and wet. And he was hungry too. You see, he wasn't carrying any food.
CLAIRE: What was the weather like?
JOCK: Terrible. It was snowing all morning and there was a strong wind. It's lucky we found him when we did.
CLAIRE: Was he hurt?
JOCK: He had a broken leg, so he couldn't move very far.
CLAIRE: How did he break his leg?
JOCK: He slipped on a wet rock and fell. He was very tired by that time.
CLAIRE: Is he all right now?
JOCK: Oh yes, he's in the hospital and he's being well looked after. He'll be all right. But he's a very lucky young man.
CLAIRE: Why do you say that?
JOCK: Because he was nearly killed. He was very foolish. He shouldn't have gone on when the storm started, he really shouldn't. He should have gone back. If you go out in weather like that, you've got to be ready for it. And he wasn't.
CLAIRE: But when he left the sun was shining.
JOCK: I know, but the weather in the mountains can change very quickly. That's why they're so dangerous.

Now mark these statements right (✓) or wrong (×):

1 The Mountain Rescue Team found David under a rock.   ✓
2 He had some food with him.   ✗
3 When they found him the weather was quite good.   ✗
4 David was hurt.   ✓
5 Jock Douglas doesn't know how David broke his leg.   ✗
6 David is in hospital.   ✓
7 When David started walking it was sunny.   ✓
8 The weather in the mountains doesn't often change quickly.   ✗

Answer this question:
9 Why does Jock think David was lucky?
Because He didn't take enough care + he was almost killed.

exposure - ausgesetzt.

Unit Sixteen

1 Regretting

You are at a party. Express regret for some of the things that happen there:

1 I'm late. — I'm sorry I'm late.

2 Clive couldn't come. — It's a pity Clive couldn't come.

3 I forgot to bring my records. — I'm sorry I forgot to bring my records.

4 I dropped that green cup. — I'm sorry I broke that green cup.

5 It broke. — It's a pity it broke.

6 Your husband was angry with me. — It's a pity your husband was angry with me.

7 I have to go now. — I'm sorry I have to go now.

2 Making suggestions

Marcia is talking to Olivia. She makes a suggestion. Olivia accepts it.

Why didn't you write to him?

You're right. I should have written to him.

You have seen a fight in the street. You tell your friend. Accept his/her suggestions:

1 Why didn't you shout?

You're right. I should have shouted.

2 Why didn't you go for help?

You're right. I should have gone for help.

3 Why didn't you help the little boy?

You're right. I should have helped him (the little boy.)

4 Why didn't you call the police?

You're right. I should have called them (the police.)

5 Why didn't you tell them about the fight?

You're right. I should have told them about it (the fight.)

Unit Sixteen

3 Crossword

All the words in this crossword appear in Unit Sixteen.

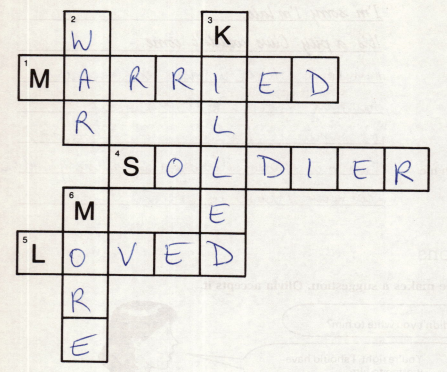

Across
1 Donald wanted to get ___married___ to Olivia.
4 He was a ___soldier___.
5 Olivia ___loved___ him.

Down
2 Donald had to fight in the ___war___.
3 He was ___killed___ in Italy.
6 Olivia was sorry they didn't have ___more___ time together.

4 Replies

(= Yes, I will *write*.)
(= No, I'm not *crying*.)

Marcia and Olivia are talking about Donald. Complete their replies:

1 Has Donald gone?   Yes, he ___has___.

2 He asked me to marry him. yesterday   ~~Has~~ Did he?

3 Did you say 'yes'?   No, ___I___ ___didn't___.

You must think I'm crazy.   No, ___I___ ___don't___.

Don't tell Edith.   No, I ___won't___.

Unit Sixteen

5 Breaking the news

Donald's family is the first to get the news of his death. Clive, Donald's brother, goes to Olivia's house to break the news. She invites him in.

CLIVE: I've got some news about Donald. I'm afraid it's bad news. If I were you, I'd sit down.
OLIVIA: Bad news? What is it? Tell me, Clive. You must tell me. What's happened?
CLIVE: We've had a telegram. I'm afraid he's been wounded. Badly wounded.
OLIVIA: (*crying*) Oh no! He's dead, isn't he? Tell me the truth.
CLIVE: He was leading his men across a bridge when it happened. Olivia, I want you to understand that he died bravely. He died like a soldier.
OLIVIA: Oh, what does that matter? Do you think I care about that? The only thing that matters is that he's dead. Donald's dead! (*sobs*)
CLIVE: I'll get you a drink.
OLIVIA: I shouldn't have let him go. I wrote him a letter, but I didn't post it. I should have posted it. Oh, why didn't I post it? (*sobs*)
CLIVE: Here, take this. You mustn't blame yourself, you know. You really mustn't.
OLIVIA: But I do blame myself. I should have married him. That's what he wanted. But I wasn't sure. I wanted to wait. I wasn't ready.
CLIVE: I'm sure you were right. You were both very young.
OLIVIA: Clive, thank you for coming round to tell me. It must have been difficult for you. Can we just talk about Donald for a bit? I think it would help me.
CLIVE: It would help me if we talked about him too. He was my brother and I loved him. (*sobs*)

Mark these statements right (✓) or wrong (✗):

1 Clive tells Olivia to sit down because she's tired. ✗
2 At first he tells her that Donald is only wounded. ✓
3 Olivia doesn't believe him. ✓
4 Olivia doesn't care that Donald is dead. ✗
5 She is sorry she didn't post her letter to Donald. ✓
6 Donald wanted to marry Olivia. ✓
7 Clive thinks Olivia and Donald should have got married. ✗
8 Olivia is grateful to Clive for coming. ✓
9 She doesn't want to talk about Donald. ✗
10 Clive wants to talk about Donald. ✓

Unit Seventeen

1 If I won a million...

Claire Walton asked three people what they would do if they won a million pounds. Here are their replies:

- I'd buy a boat and sail round the world in it.
- I'd buy a nice house and a big car. Then I'd put the rest of the money in the bank.
- I'd give it away to a charity. I don't want as much money as that. It only causes trouble.

Now write about what *you* would do if you won a million pounds. Here are some questions to think about before you write:

Would you stop work? If so, what would you do?

Would you spend all the money or save some?

What would you do if people asked you for money?

2 Fix these sentences

These sentences have been broken into two parts. For each sentence (1–5) find the second part (a–e) which goes with it; then write out the sentence in full. For example:

1/d If I could cook, I'd bake you a birthday cake.

1 If I could cook,
2 If I were you,
3 If I were a film star,
4 If I had to live in another country,
5 If I stopped work,

a I wouldn't buy that dress.
b I'd choose Australia.
c I'd be bored.
d I'd bake you a birthday cake.
e I'd live in Hollywood.

Unit Seventeen

3 Party talk

Here are pictures taken at the party. What do you think these people are saying? Choose from the sentences given below:

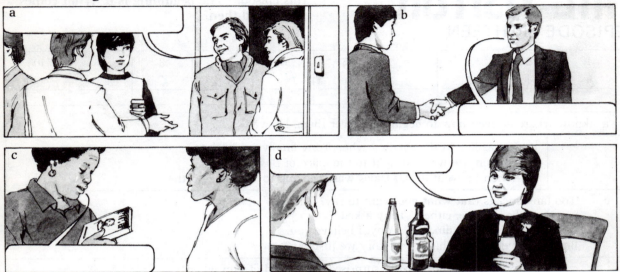

1 I'm looking forward to reading this book. 2 Why don't we go outside? 3 It's late. We must go. 4 Pleased to meet you. 5 Can I take your coat? 6 Would you like red or white wine?

a _3_   b _4_   c _1_   d _6_

4 Complete the conversation

Use a form of the verbs in brackets to complete this conversation:

1 I've just (*go*) back to work. — _gone_

2 I've (*start*) (*teach*) again. — _started teaching_

3 I'm looking forward to (*work*) again. — _working_

4 That's interesting. I used (*be*) a teacher. — _to be_

5 I'm afraid I (*not enjoy*) it very much. — _I'm not enjoying_

6 I hated (*get up*) early. — _getting up_

7 I used to look forward to (*stop*) work every day. — _stopping_

51

Unit Seventeen

5 Jigsaw reading

THE VISITOR
EPISODE EIGHTEEN

What is the correct order of the ten parts of this episode? The beginning is b. What comes next? And then?

1	2	3	4	5	6	7	8	9	10
b	d	h	a	j	f	i	c	g	e

a   know where or even how to begin to answer them. He was

b   It was late in the evening when Tony finally got back to London. He went straight to the office of *Business News*. When he went in, Liz Davis was speaking to someone on the

c   'Too fantastic? Is that what you want to say? That you don't believe me, either?' Tony asked.
Liz shook her head again. 'No, Tony. I believe you. But nobody else will. This is one story we just can't

d   phone. She looked very surprised and stared at him when she saw him. 'My God, Tony! Where have you been? Don't you know that the police have been looking for you everywhere?' she asked. Tony sat down without a

e   at the dark sky. He could see a bright star in the east. He stared at it for a long time.
'I wonder if I'll ever see her again?' he finally said.
'Who?' Liz asked.
'Tan-Lin, of course,' Tony answered.

f   like some coffee?' she asked. Tony nodded. Then he slowly began to tell her the whole story. Liz

g   print,' she answered.
'No, of course you can't. I understand that,' Tony said.
He got up and went over to the window, too. He looked up

h   word and held his head in his hands. Liz immediately began to ask him all sorts of questions but Tony didn't

i   listened in silence, puffing her cigarette. When he finished, she shook her head and walked to the window. She began to speak but couldn't finish.
'Your story is just too . . . too . . .,'

j   very tired.
'What's wrong with you? What's happened?' she asked.
'You just wouldn't believe me if I told you,' he answered.
Liz lit another cigarette and stared at him. 'Would you